C000203591

BRITAIN IN OLD P

AROUND HAYES
AND WEST
DRAYTON

EDITED BY

PHILIP SHERWOOD

SUTTON PUBLISHING LIMITED

First published in 1996 by
Sutton Publishing Limited
Phoenix Mill · Thrupp · Stroud
Gloucestershire · GL5 2BU

British Library Cataloguing in Publication Data
A catalogue record for this book is available from the
British Library.

ISBN 0-7509-1036-4

Typeset in 10/12 Perpetua.
Typesetting and origination by
Sutton Publishing Limited.
Printed in Great Britain by
Ebenezer Baylis, Worcester.

Dedicated to the memory of John Hammond and of Archie Cox. John contributed much to the photographic collection of the Hayes & Harlington Local History Society. Archie was a founder member of the West Drayton & District Local History Society and its Chairman from 1955 to 1983.

Philip Sherwood was born in Sipson but now lives in Harlington where, on his mother's side, his family has lived for many generations. He was educated at Bishopshalt Grammar School and later at Birkbeck College of the University of London where he obtained a degree in Chemistry. He is a chemist by profession and is a Fellow of the Royal Society of Chemistry. As a Principal Scientific Officer in the Scientific Civil Service he has worked at the Transport (formerly Road) Research Laboratory and the Royal Commission on Environmental Pollution, but now works as a self-employed consultant.

He has written many articles and books on the local history of the Harmondsworth/Harlington area and lectures extensively on the subject. He has been the Treasurer of the Hayes & Harlington Local History for many years and is also the Hillingdon area representative for the London Branch of the Council for the Protection of Rural England.

CONTENTS

Town Hall, Yiewsley, 27 September 1939. The Town Hall was opened in 1930 and is shown here protected by sandbags, soon after the start of the Second World War.

ACKNOWLEDGEMENTS

Except where otherwise stated, all the photographs are from negatives or originals owned by either the Hayes and Harlington Local History Society, the West Drayton and District Local History Society or P.T. Sherwood. Grateful thanks are due, however, to the various individuals who have donated or loaned for copying the original photographs, postcards and paintings, which have been reproduced here. These include Miss A. Glenie, the late Mrs A.L.E. Moore, Mrs R. Pearce, Mrs A. Swann, the late Mrs F.M. Symmons, the late Mrs M. Wild, Mr B. Cockram, Major D. Francombe, the late Mr C. Hammond, Mr J. Hearne, Mr S.J. Heyward, Mr A. Prince, Mr D.M. Rust, and Mr W. Wild. Particular acknowledgement should be made to the late Mr John Hammond (1942–95), Secretary of the Hayes and Harlington Local History Society until his untimely death. Over a period of many years, he acquired a unique collection of picture postcards and photographs which he made freely available for the Society to copy and many of the photographs of Hayes and Harlington come from his collection.

INTRODUCTION

The photographs in this book were, for the most part, taken in the period 1890–1940 in the area around Hayes and West Drayton which also includes Yiewsley, Harlington and Harmondsworth (with Sipson, Longford and Heathrow). They recall a rural past of peaceful Middlesex villages which is well within the memory of many people still living in an area which has changed beyond recognition in their lifetime. This peaceful way of life was shattered for ever in 1944 with the development of Heathrow airport. The hamlet of Heathrow was obliterated and the very existence of Harlington, and that of the villages of Harmondsworth parish immediately to the north of the airport, has been under continual threat from further development for the past fifty years. Even in those parts further away from the airport there has been a change from traditional industries to airport-related uses. The photographs in the book graphically reflect the changes that have occurred, and are still occurring.

The area covered is now that part of the London Borough of Hillingdon which is south of the Uxbridge Road (A4040) but it excludes Uxbridge and Cowley, which are the subject of another book in this series. However, at the time that most of the photographs were taken, Harlington and Harmondsworth parishes were both part of Staines Rural District whilst Hayes, West Drayton and Yiewsley formed part of Uxbridge Rural District. Urbanization of the area began around Hayes and Yiewsley, mainly as a result of their good communications with London via the Grand Junction Canal and the Great Western Railway. Hayes became an Urban District in 1904 and Yiewsley in 1911. Further reorganization in 1930 created the Urban Districts of Yiewsley and West Drayton (which included Harmondsworth parish) and of Hayes and Harlington. These were further amalgamated in 1965, with Uxbridge and Ruislip, to form the London Borough of Hillingdon.

P.T. Sherwood
Harlington, 1996

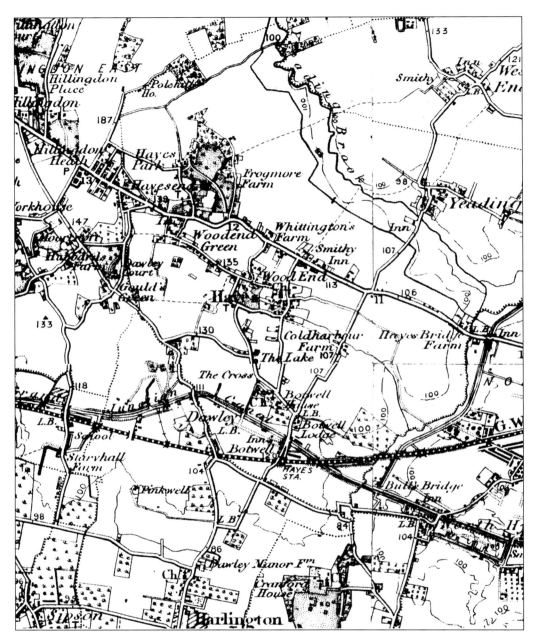

Hayes, *c.* 1900. Hayes Village, then known as Hayes Town or Cotman Town, lies roughly in the centre of the large parish of Hayes. Around it are the still separate hamlets of Hayes End, Wood End, Wood End Green and, in the extreme south of the parish, Botwell, which has since usurped the name Hayes Town. More remote to the north-east is the outlying hamlet of Yeading where, according to a nineteenth-century chronicler, 'Dirt, ignorance and darkness reigned supreme'.

SECTION ONE

HAYES

Church Green, Hayes Town, c. 1910. Church Green lay at the centre of Hayes Town, the village of Hayes. In the background on the right is the tower of the parish church of St Mary, while on the left is Hayes Court or Court Farm. The timber-framed and weatherboarded cottages, with a brick extension at the rear, were probably eighteenth century. To the photographer's left, out of shot, were the village lock-up, the cattle pound and the fire engine shed, while behind him stood the Manor House. All the buildings except the church have now gone and the pond has been filled in; this peaceful spot today tends to be dominated by parked cars.

Hayes Court, Church Green, *c.* 1967. Court Farm was probably once the manorial demesne, although it had already ceased to be so by 1766 when it was purchased by William Minet. The main part of the house (on the right), was of late eighteenth- or early nineteenth-century construction although the west wing and out-buildings were probably earlier. The house was demolished in 1968.

Hayes Manor House, Church Road, 1934. The Manor of Hayes was in the possession of the Archbishop of Canterbury before the Reformation. Surviving traces of a moat probably mark the site of the previous medieval manor house but the earliest part of the building shown here (to the left facing north) was sixteenth century; this part was destroyed by fire in 1939. The remaining part dates from the seventeenth century but Henry Boot, a previous owner and a builder by trade, made drastic alterations including modernizing the plumbing and adding the neo-Tudor timber-framing at the west end.

Hayes Town, *c.* 1900. Despite pressure from developers, the village street has managed to retain something of its character. The top photograph, looking north, shows on the left the entrance to the Hayes Laundry, four tiny cottages and The Old Queen's Head on the corner of Church Green. To the right is Wistowe House (seventeenth to nineteenth century), and next to it Barden House and Little Barden, named after the nineteenth-century landowner. The shop beyond was formerly a grocer's and later a butcher's, and was replaced in 1904 by the present building. The bottom photograph, looking south, shows Hayes Town Chapel on the right; founded in 1788, it was enlarged in the nineteenth century and demolished in 1959. Next to the chapel can be seen Craven House, with the old Royal Oak public house in the distance. On the left, behind the tree, is Cotman Lodge, named from the alternative name for the village, Cotman Town.

Calf Provision Merchant and Family Grocer's shop, *c.* 1900. This stood on the east side of the village street in Hayes Town. The business was started by Robert Calf and was continued by his widow Ann who, from 1887, also ran a post office on the premises. By 1906 the shop was owned by Platt's Stores Ltd. Part of Porch House, a late Georgian building, can be seen behind the shop. This was demolished about 1915 and a row of four cottages, known as Porch Houses, was built on the site.

Rear view of the Rectory, Hayes Town, *c.* 1913. In 1910 two houses, 'The Briars' (left) and 'The Hawthorns', which had both been built by Seth Hunt about 1904, were converted into one and leased for use as the Rectory. In about 1916 the building was converted back to two dwellings and 'The Hawthorns' became a small private school at which Eric Blair came to teach in 1932-3. He was also a writer and during his time at the school he adopted the pen-name George Orwell. Both buildings are now reunited as the Fountain House Hotel.

Manor Lodge, Freeman's Lane, 1936. Manor Lodge was the last name given to this building before it was demolished in 1949. Originally the Vicarage, it was built by the Rector of Hayes in about 1520. It was later used as the Rector's residence until about 1860 when the Rector was permitted by the Church Commissioners to renovate the old Manor House for use as the Rectory. The Vicarage was then, confusingly, renamed Manor House and occupied by E.R. Spearman and his wife, Lady Maria, daughter of the 5th Earl of Orkney. The south, and probably the original part of the house, is shown here; the west wing with its Dutch gables was apparently altered in about 1640.

No. 18 Freeman's Lane, 1961. This building was erected in about 1830 by the Hunt family for use as a Sunday School by the congregation of Hayes Town Chapel. It was brick-built at ground level and timber-framed and weatherboarded above. It later became a private residence and was lived in by the Gibbons family; in November 1884 Mrs Gibbons murdered her husband here. Demolition of this and all the other old cottages in Freeman's Lane began in 1959.

Peace celebrations, Wood End, 9 August 1919. The end of the First World War, in which 93 Hayes servicemen died, was celebrated in the following year. A procession marched around Hayes from Clayton Road via Station Road and Uxbridge Road to Wood End, where a fairground had been set up with a roundabout and swings and other entertainments. (*See* p. 18)

Hayes Cricket Club, Wood End, 1956. Although photographed as late as 1956 in highly industrialized Hayes, this is a typical village scene. A match is in progress against a backdrop of the parish church (centre) and the buildings of Dr Triplett's school in Church Walk on the right. The cricket ground is still used today but the school buildings were demolished in 1969 after a new school was built, not far away, in Hemmen Lane.

Wood End and Wood End House. In the photograph above, taken in 1905 looking north, Wood End House is partly hidden behind the trees with the coachman's or gardener's cottage to its left. To the left of the pond is a pair of cottages (Hearn's Cottages) which may originally have been one farmhouse. They were demolished in 1952. The photograph below shows Wood End House in 1961, shortly before it was demolished. This house was believed to have been a hunting lodge built during the reign of Henry VIII. The east wing (right) was the oldest part and may have had sixteenth-century foundations. The west wing was added later, while the (hidden) north wing was late eighteenth or early nineteenth century.

Barra Hall, Wood End, *c.* 1933. In the late eighteenth century Grove House was the home of Alderman Harvey Coombe, later Lord Mayor of London. In about 1871 the house was bought by Robert Reid, an auctioneer and surveyor, who claimed descent from the Reids of Barra; he refaced the building in a Jacobean-cum-Scottish baronial style and changed the name to Barra Hall. After his death his son sold the house to a foundation of Anglican nuns. It was eventually bought by Hayes UDC and became the Town Hall.

The Chestnuts, Wood End, 1963. This photograph typifies the sad state that has befallen most of the older and more interesting houses in Hayes. The Chestnuts' most famous occupant, from about 1788 to 1796, was Stephen Storace, the author of many light operas and a friend of Mozart and Haydn. The house was originally a simple, flat-fronted Georgian building but was extended later on the right, and a wing was added at the rear in Victorian times. Around the turn of the nineteenth century, the windows were fashionably 'Gothicized'. The last owner of the house was the local council, which demolished it in 1963.

Wood End, *c.* 1910. This village scene shows the Black Horse public house to the right, with beyond it Church Walk, leading eastwards towards Dr Triplett's school and the church. On the left are Grange Cottages which may have dated back to the eighteenth century; they had been demolished by the early 1930s.

The Queen's Head, Wood End Green Road, 1939. The little beer house in the foreground probably started life as a cottage in the eighteenth century. Although the Black Horse at Wood End was only about 100 yds away and there were two pubs in Hayes Town, the great increase in the population of Hayes in the 1920s and '30s justified the building of a new and very much larger Queens Head behind the beerhouse; the original building was then demolished. Even the name has now disappeared as the pub has now been refurbished and renamed The Grange.

Cromwell's Cottages, Wood End Green Road, *c.* 1910. Robert Cromwell, in his will of 1720, gave two houses and a barn to be rented out, the yearly revenue from which was to be used to purchase six gowns for poor women. In 1895 the rent was 2*s* 6*d* for each cottage; they were described as being 'somewhat dilapidated' and were to be repaired. However, by 1925 a closing order was put on them by the council and the Hayes Amalgamated Charities, which was responsible for them, auctioned them in 1926. They were bought for £430 by Mr Salter, a builder, who demolished them and built nos 86–96 Wood End Green Road on the site.

Wood End Green Road, *c.* 1910. On the right is Rosedale Farm House; beyond it Angel Lane leads off to the right. The row of cottages and small houses beyond are of various dates between the seventeenth and nineteenth centuries. Beyond them is Morgans Lane, also leading to the right. All these buildings have since been demolished and there is now a roundabout at the Angel Lane junction.

Wood End Green Farm, *c.* 1921. Little is known of the history of this farmhouse, which stood at the end of Wood End Green Road, although it appears to date from the eighteenth century. In 1899 the farmer was A.E. Goddard; by 1904 Mrs Goddard (presumably his widow) was running the Wood End Green Farm Dairy. It passed through several hands before being demolished soon after 1928.

Uxbridge Road, Hayes End, *c.* 1920. London United Tramways extended their line from Southall through Hayes to Uxbridge in 1904, bringing about development of this part of Hayes near the Uxbridge Road. The terrace of cottages on the left included the post office and newsagent's run by Miss Matthews, and the police station at the far end. Beyond is the single-storey butcher's shop of W. Wicks, with his house adjoining it on the corner of Hayes End Road.

Messrs W. Wicks & Son, butchers and graziers, 1938. Taken just before Christmas, this photograph shows the enticing display (no doubt horrifying to today's public health officers) of meat and poultry for Christmas dinner tables.

Peace celebrations, Uxbridge Road, 1919. This photograph was taken from a high viewpoint, perhaps from the top of a tram, looking east from near the corner of Hayes End Road. The procession was part of the peace celebrations in Hayes and was headed by the Uxbridge and Hillingdon Band, with numerous local organizations marching behind accompanied by floats representing local industry and commerce. The celebrations ended with sports and a fair at Wood End (*see* p. 12).

The Angel, Uxbridge Road, Hayes End, 1926. This old inn was just one of many on the busy stagecoach route from London to Oxford and beyond. It was demolished in 1926 to make way for the present building.

Hayes End House, 1926. This house, with pleasure grounds including a lake, apparently dated from the mid- to late eighteenth century. In the 1820s and 1830s it was the home of a local benefactor, the Hon. Juliana Curzon (1773–1835), daughter of Lord Curzon of Kedleston. By 1861 the house was described in the census as a private establishment for the education of Indian children. The school appeared to have been founded following the Indian Mutiny for the children of Catherine, Lady Ulick-Browne and those of her relatives whose fathers were senior officials in India, where most of the children were born. The school had closed by 1865, and the house was renamed The Shrubbery. It was demolished after the Second World War.

Nos 19–29 Hayes End Terrace, 1959. This single terrace of houses shows an interesting variation in styles of nineteenth-century domestic dwellings. Nos 21 and 23 (second and third from the left) were called Springwell Mount and were probably the oldest, perhaps built in the 1840s. Next to these were nos 25 and 27, added in about 1870. The terrace was completed by the addition of no. 19 at one end and no. 29 at the other. The latter both have the decorative barge-boards that were popular in Victorian times. No. 19 was dated 1882 and bore the initials of the builder, W. Hunt.

Former estate cottages, Hayes End Road, 1970. These are typical of the well built dwellings erected by some landowners for their tenants or workers. In this case the landowner was Sir Charles Mills Bt, and the cottages bear his initials and the date 1871. Attention to detail is demonstrated by the patterned fish-scale tiles, the barge-boards and the string course of different coloured bricks. Following the death in 1919 of Sir Charles Mills' grandson, the second Lord Hillingdon, the Hillingdon Court Estate was sold. At this time the cottages were part of Hayes End Farm.

Hayes Park, Hayes End, *c*. 1905. Robert Willis Blencowe had a farmhouse on this site in 1813 and the house shown here is a rebuilding or enlargement of it. In 1829 Blencowe became Lord of the Manor. His son inherited the Hayes estate in 1842; he lived in Sussex but his sister and her husband occupied the house for some years. By 1851 it had been taken over for use as a private lunatic asylum for men, then for men and women and later for females only. This lasted until H.J. Heinz Ltd, food manufacturers, bought the estate in 1959 for use as head offices and a food research centre. They demolished the mansion house in 1962.

Hayes Cottage Hospital, Grange Road, *c*. 1906. The hospital was built in 1875 to replace an earlier, much smaller, hospital elsewhere in Hayes. The money for building the hospital was raised by subscription and the foundation stone was laid on 6 April 1875 by Mrs Godding, wife of the Rector of Hayes. When the Hayes UDC vacated a building a short distance to the north, it was acquired for the hospital in 1926, and was joined to the original building by a new wing.

Corinth Parade, Uxbridge Road, *c.* 1950. This parade of shops takes its name from the cinema on the right. Behind the shops lies the Grange Park Estate, consisting of 1,200 dwellings; built in the early 1930s by Frank Taylor this could, perhaps, be claimed to be the foundation of the giant Taylor–Woodrow enterprise. In 1933 Taylor also built the Corinth Cinema which was renamed the Essoldo after the Second World War, and was eventually demolished to be replaced by a tower block.

Crown Parade, Uxbridge Road, 1944. This was the scene shortly after a German V2 rocket had fallen behind the shops on Gledwood Drive at 1.15 a.m. on 21 October 1944. It created a 50 ft crater and did much damage although, surprisingly, no one was killed. There were, however, 16 serious and 41 minor casualties. Some houses had to be demolished and replaced later, but the shops were repaired. In general, Hayes suffered relatively lightly from aerial attack, although a V1 flying bomb that hit a Gramophone Company surface air-raid shelter in 1944 caused 37 deaths and numerous injuries.

The Adam and Eve public house, Uxbridge Road, 1904. This was once a coaching inn with extensive stables and lodgings for grooms, ostlers and so on in the yard behind. The stagecoach trade had long gone by 1904 but the extension of the tramway service along the Uxbridge Road in this year brought some compensation in the form of day-trippers visiting the countryside. The house to the left of the inn, called Oakdene, was the home of a suffragist, Marion Cunningham, from at least 1907. The old Adam and Eve was replaced by a new pub in 1937 and Oakdene is now a fast food outlet.

Adam and Eve pond, c. 1905. This view would have been enjoyed by those drinking their pints outside the pub. The pond was used for watering cattle and horses, and possibly also by the drivers of steam traction engines, such as the one shown here. The road ahead (now Church Road) leads to the village and the church tower can be seen between the trees.

Haymaking near the Uxbridge Road, *c.* 1900. The men are resting from their labours in a meadow that probably belonged to Court Farm. The Cottage Hospital (*see* p. 21) can be seen in the distance, over the horse's rump. Much of this area is now taken up by the Beck Theatre and its associated car-parks.

Rectory Farm, Uxbridge Road, *c.* 1900. The cart's load consists of thatching reeds which appear to have been entered in a competition because a card, inscribed Second Prize, is attached to them. The cart bears the name Jason Wilshin, Hayes; he was a member of a prominent family in the district who also farmed at Rectory Farm.

The Blue Pool, Uxbridge Road, *c*. 1935. This public open-air swimming pool was greatly enjoyed on hot summer days. However, such pools are at the mercy of our unpredictable climate and, later, most tended to be enclosed. The pool closed in 1938 when the Savoy Cinema was constructed on its site.

Brickmaking, Uxbridge Road, *c*. 1905. The Grand Junction Canal from Brentford to Uxbridge was opened through Hayes in 1794 and completed to Braunston, Northants., in 1805. The Paddington Arm of the canal opened in 1801. The presence of brick-earth deposits adjacent to the canal between Yiewsley, Dawley, Hayes and Yeading led to the establishment of brickworks in these areas which supplied bricks taken by water to the London market. This photograph was taken on the south side of the Uxbridge Road close to the boundary with Southall; between 1901 and 1960 it was worked by the East Acton Brickworks Company. The men and boys are posing with the tools of their trade; the man standing at the extreme left is George Leather.

Poplar Farm, Yeading Lane, *c.* 1925. Here the cows are being driven over Yeading Lane, which runs across the middle of the picture, to their sheds at Poplar Farm, just to the north of the junction with Willow Tree Lane. The fields shown here and, more recently, the brickfields and rubbish dumps east of Yeading Lane, have been built over almost as far as the canal.

Barn, Yeading Manor Farm, Yeading Fork, 1961. The Manor of Yeading was quite distinct from that of Hayes. Its earliest recorded lord was the Bishop of Lichfield and Coventry in 1307. Five hundred years later the manor belonged to the Revd John Louis Petit who built a new house there in 1848. This became the farmhouse of Manor Farm which lay to the east of Yeading Fork. The farm buildings included this magnificent barn nearly 110 ft in length. A year after the photograph was taken all the farm buildings were demolished.

Converted railway carriage, Willow Tree Lane, Yeading *c*. 1930. This type of dwelling was more normally associated with the seaside than with inland counties, but dwellings like this, cheap, pre-fabricated (obviously!) and easily transported and set up, were popular in the 1920s and '30s. It is not known when it was removed.

The Willow Tree public house, Jolly's Lane, Yeading, 1957. At this time the pub was in an isolated spot, with only a few cottages nearby and semi-derelict land behind it stretching back to the Grand Union Canal. The pub is believed to have been built about 1840, almost certainly to cater for workers in the local brickfields. Barges took the bricks to London and returned with rubbish which was used to infill the worked-out excavations. The whole area is now covered by housing.

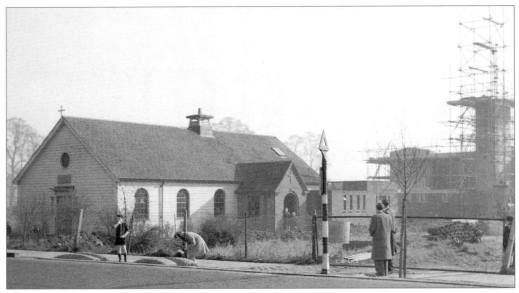

The church of St Edmund, Yeading Lane, 1961. The expanding population of the parish of Hayes after the First World War led, first of all, to the creation of a separate parish of St Anselm at Botwell, in the southern part of Hayes. Other sub-parishes were also formed, including that of St Edmund at Yeading in 1932. The first church was little more than a small single-storey shed, which was replaced in 1933 with a much larger building; this survived until the opening of the present church, which was consecrated by the Bishop of Kensington on 1 July 1961. The photograph shows the new church being built behind the 1933 church.

Coldharbour Farm House, Coldharbour Lane, 1956. This farmhouse was said to have a brick dated 1720, which is probably when it was built, although a nineteenth-century extension was added at the rear. The greater part of the land belonging to the farm ran from the Uxbridge Road down to where Minet Drive is today and eastward to Yeading Brook. The farmhouse has since been demolished.

Little Dawley, Church Road, 1961. A short way south of the village on the road to Botwell, this house had a brick dated 1787 on its south gable end. In the early 1930s George Orwell's pupils from The Hawthorns (*see* p. 10) used the grounds to play cricket. Later the house was acquired by the local Conservative Association which demolished it in 1973.

Belle House, Botwell Lane, *c.* 1962. A building which pre-dated 1816, Belle (or Bell) House was a private dwelling that by 1841 had become a boys' school, run by Joseph Fleet, with 37 pupils aged between 7 and 13 years. It remained as a school until at least 1881, when T. Hales was the proprietor, after which it was a private residence again. In the 1930s the house became a Roman Catholic convent; it was demolished when the present convent was built in 1962.

The Golden Cross public house, Botwell Lane, c. 1912. This building was a typical mid-nineteenth-century pub which has now been replaced with a modern building on the same site. The licensee in 1912 was Mrs Mostyn, who was presumably the widow of the former licensee, Frederick George Mostyn.

The Botwell housing estate, October 1920. The Hayes UDC had built a few houses just before the First World War, but the demand for accommodation created by the huge influx of war workers into the local factories led to an acute shortage of housing. This prompted the Council to embark on a large housing scheme, under the Housing and Town Planning Act of 1919. The site chosen was a triangular area bounded roughly by Church Road, Uxbridge Road and Coldharbour Lane. The first part of the Council's plan was for 766 houses and building was well under way when this photograph was taken. To facilitate the movement of materials around the site, a light railway was built from the GWR main line with its own bridge across the line.

Aerial view of Botwell, *c.* 1932. This interesting photograph shows the mixture of industry, agriculture and housing in the southern part of Hayes. In the foreground is the Great Western railway line and north of this, running diagonally across the centre of the photograph, is the Grand Union (formerly Grand Junction) Canal linking London with the Midlands; these two transport systems were largely instrumental in attracting manufacturing industry to the Botwell area of Hayes. At the extreme left can be seen some of the buildings of the Gramophone Company and, just left of centre, the factory premises of the British Electric Transformer Company in Clayton Road; north of the canal is the printing works of Harrison & Sons. In Clayton Road and Blyth Road (south of Clayton Road) some of the houses built at the same time as the factories can be seen. On the right is Station Road, with shops on both sides, the newly built St Anselm's Church and the post office to its north. Further up the road is the large building of the Methodist Queen's Hall and beyond it, curving round to the left, is Botwell Lane with Botwell House and its Roman Catholic chapel. In the distance on the left is Botwell Common while to the right a small part of the Botwell housing estate can be seen.

Station Road, Botwell *c.* 1954. The presence of the canal and railway encouraged the establishment of factories in their vicinity and the commercial centre of Hayes shifted to Botwell. Shops sprang up in Station Road and along Botwell Lane (to the right, beyond the telephone kiosk) and Coldharbour Lane (in the foreground). At this time the larger shops included a branch of Burton's the tailors. Among other buildings were the Queen's Hall Methodist Church and the Regent Cinema which opened in 1924. It became a theatre in 1948 but closed in 1953.

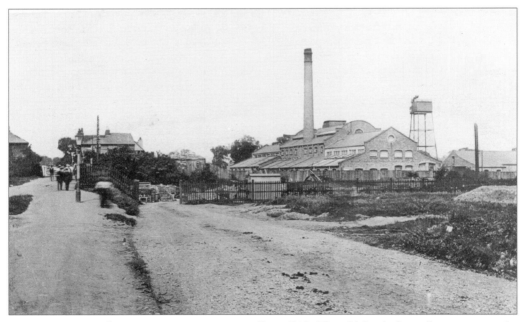

Harrison & Sons Ltd, Printing House Lane, Botwell, *c.* 1912. This old family firm of printers won the post office contract in 1910 for the supply of postage stamps. They acquired a new factory, on the north bank of the canal, which had formerly made fire-proof boards. Production of stamps started in early 1911 and after the GPO contract was lost in 1923, the firm branched out into other printing activities. The factory closed in the 1970s when Harrisons moved out of the district.

Station Road, Botwell. The top photograph was taken looking north over the canal bridge in about 1913.On the extreme right is The Old Crown, a Victorian pub, with a row of shops called York House to its left. The Hayes Cinema, a long white building, the roof of which can just be seen, opened in 1913 and closed only three years later. The bottom photograph was taken looking south in about 1920. The nearest buildings are Glyn Cottages with, on the corner of Clayton Road (leading off to the right), a sub-branch of the London, City and Midland Bank which opened only one day a week. Among the other cottages are the 'Railway Toilet Saloon', a watchmaker's and jeweller's, and the newsagents shop of F.W. Hilliar. The taller pair of houses, known as Surrey House, contained the shops of a boot repairer and C.E. Gaylard, pharmacist.

Clayton Road, Botwell. The top photograph shows workers leaving the factory of the Army Motor Lorries and Waggon Co. in 1915. The factory was taken over for the purpose of making and repairing vehicles for the Belgian Army, since the industrial parts of Belgium were under German occupation. Many refugee Belgians were employed by the company. In 1915 part of the premises was taken over by the Fairey Aviation Company. Disputes between the two companies ceased when the Belgian company went bankrupt. The Fairey Aviation Company was formed in 1915 by Richard Fairey and its first contracts were for the assembly of Short and Sopwith aircraft. Fairey's own first design was the F2, but his greatest achievement was an adaptation of a Sopwith Baby seaplane. This had a patent system for adjusting the wing trailing edge flaps as a means of increasing lift for take-off and landing. The prototype Hamble Baby, as it was called, is shown in the bottom photograph in the Clayton Road factory in 1916.

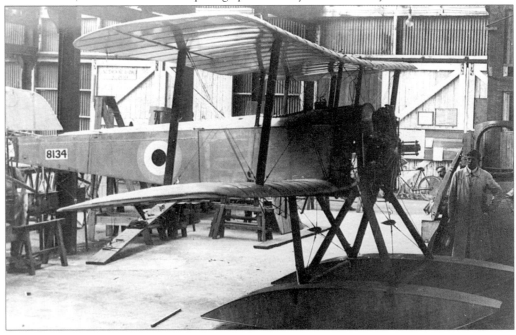

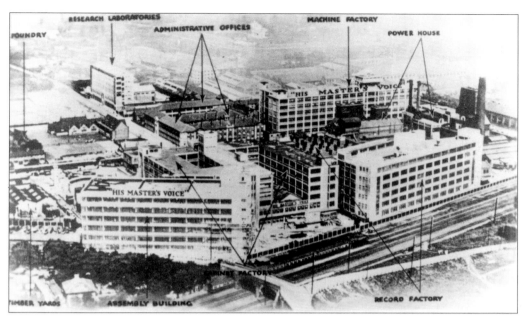

The EMI factory complex, Blyth Road, 1934. This aerial photograph, looking north-east, was taken for a publicity postcard. The company, which began life in 1898 as The Gramophone (and Typewriter) Company, moved to Hayes in 1907 where it made, and still makes, recordings under the His Master's Voice and other labels. It greatly expanded its activities and, after taking over the Columbia Gramophone Company in 1931, changed its name to Electric and Musical Industries (EMI). During the Second World War EMI's war work included radar development and manufacture. Copies of this photograph were reproduced by the Germans and given to Luftwaffe bomber pilots as target information.

Council School, Clayton Road, c. 1910. The Hayes Development Company, in developing the industrial site between the canal and the railway at Botwell, made provision for a school to serve the increased population and a Council School was opened in 1906. The roll had increased from 134 to 732 by 1927, but new Council and other housing estates had by then shifted the population centre further north. The school closed in 1931 and was sold to EMI which demolished it in 1962.

Sandow's Cocoa and Chocolate Company, Sandow Road (Nestles Avenue), Botwell c. 1915. This company was founded by the amazing Eugene Sandow, the legendary strongman of the music hall. He could lift over his head a grand piano whilst it was being played and once fought a lion and won! After retiring from the stage he opened several physical culture centres. He convinced himself of the value of cocoa as a health food and so decided to manufacture cocoa. A 42 acre site at Botwell was purchased and the factory completed in 1914. He ran into financial difficulties and the factory was taken over, as the Hayes Cocoa Company, by another company in 1916; this in turn was absorbed by Nestlés in 1929.

The Aeolian Company, Silverdale Road, Botwell, c. 1928. This company held the patents for the Pianola mechanical piano player, and completed a four-storey piano factory in 1909. Other blocks were added, including a new six-storey factory about 1922. The company and its subsidiaries were by then making gramophones and gramophone records (as rivals to EMI), as well as pianos, player pianos and music rolls. A long industrial dispute followed by serious financial irregularities resulted eventually in the closure of the factory cottages.

WEST DRAYTON

*West Drayton post office, The Green, c. 1905. Built in the
seventeenth century, this building became the village shop and post
office. In 1766 the business was bought by John Haynes and it
remained in his family until shortly after the Second World War.
The shop continued under various owners until 1972, when the
premises were converted into a private residence. (See p. 46.)*

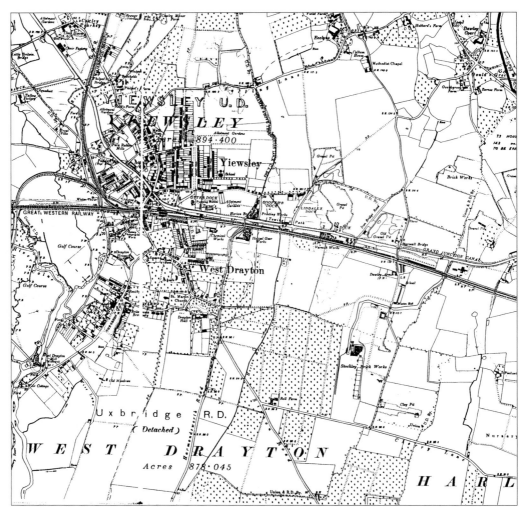

West Drayton and Yiewsley, *c.* 1912. By this time Yiewsley and West Drayton had already merged, with the railway line acting as a convenient boundary between the two. To the south much open land remains between West Drayton and Harmondsworth and Sipson respectively, both of which are just off the map. To the east lie the brick-fields of Stockley which started operations soon after the opening of the Grand Junction Canal, which provided good transport between the brickfields and the London market.

St Martin's Church. There has been a church on this site since Saxon times but the present building dates from the mid-fifteenth century, incorporating a few parts of some thirteenth-century work at the base of the tower. The top photograph shows the church before the ivy was removed and the building restored in the late 1920s. The bottom photograph shows the church in the 1930s with the Gatehouse (*see* p. 45) to the left.

Footbridge over the River Colne, early 1900s. After the Second World War the footbridge was replaced by a Bailey Bridge which can be used by motor vehicles. West Drayton Mill can be seen in the background to the left.

West Drayton Mill, *c*. 1900. Originally a corn mill, by 1559 the complex housed two corn mills and a malt mill but by 1696 it had become largely a paper mill. In 1796 it was leased to Nicholas Mercer who rebuilt the mill in about 1800; by 1876 it was described as the largest millboard mill in existence. The mill was badly damaged by fire in 1904.

West Drayton Mill, 1913. The mill survived a fire in 1904 but it was destroyed by a later fire on 9 February 1913. It was never rebuilt. The Mill House, shown on the right of the top photograph, survived the fire, but the mill itself was gutted, as shown in the bottom photograph. The ruins were left largely untouched for more than eighty years before the site was redeveloped and the Mill House restored. The top photograph shows Harmondsworth fire brigade at the scene (*see* p.101).

The local fire brigade with its new fire engine, *c*. 1937. The fire service came under the control of the Yiewsley and West Drayton UDC when it took over responsibility for the administration of West Drayton, Yiewsley and Harmondsworth.

Weir Cottage, *c*. 1930. This cottage stood between the rivers Colne and Frays, near the spot where they rejoin. In the nineteenth century it was used as a fishing lodge by the De Burgh family. It was destroyed by fire in the 1940s.

Drayton House, *c.* 1910. The house on this site, formerly known as The Burroughs, was the manor house of the Manor of Drayton or Colham Garden. It dated from the seventeenth century and was demolished in 1923.

Drayton Hall, 1925. In the nineteenth century this was the home of the De Burgh family, Lords of the Manor of West Drayton from 1786 to 1939. In 1872 Hubert de Burgh entertained Napoleon III here. Although the Hall remained in the possession of the family until 1931, it was often let to tenants and in 1925 it was a private hotel. It later became council offices, firstly of the UDC and later of Hillingdon Council, which sold it in the 1980s. It is now used as office accommodation by United Biscuits.

Staff and pupils of Beaufort House School at Vine House, West Drayton Green, *c*. 1886. This was a private school for boys of preparatory school age. The only local boy in the group was W. Guy Mercer (1880–1912), seated in the middle of the front row.

West Drayton National School was a Church of England school dating from 1859. It closed in about 1950 and the building was demolished in 1961 to provide the site for the new West Drayton Library where the school name plaque is incorporated in a boundary wall.

The Gatehouse, *c.* 1910. The Gatehouse is all that remains of the Manor House of Sir William Paget (1505–63), later 1st Baron Paget of Beaudesart, but parts of the wall surrounding the estate survive in Church Road. The houses on the left were under construction at the time of the 1881 Census.

Blacksmith's shop, Swan Road, *c.* 1910. There was a smithy on this site in 1824 and this is probably the same building.

The Green, *c*. 1905. The top photograph shows the eastern side. The building on the left is the post office and village store which had been owned by the Haynes family since 1766. Beyond is Thatcher's Britannia Brewery and Brewery Tap which closed in 1911. The large house is Elmsdale, a nineteenth-century residence, and beyond that is Swift's drapers shop and the terrace of Daisy Villas built in 1896. The bottom photograph shows the western side. Rumble's bakery on the left adjoins St Catherine's Church and survives as a shop. The Crown Inn was demolished in 1924 and Rumble's new shop was built on the site. The Swan Inn can be seen in the background.

The Swan, Swan Road. The Swan Inn and the adjoining buildings, thought to date from the sixteenth century, were demolished in 1964-5, and the inn was replaced by a modern building with the same name. The Victorian houses to the right of the inn, known as Gothic Villas, have survived.

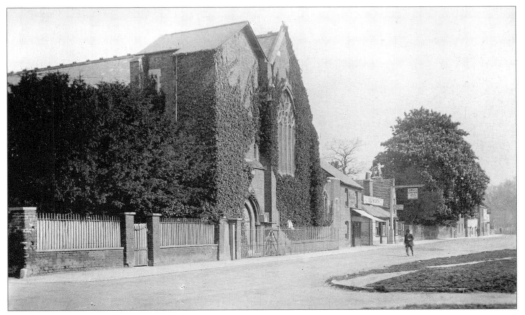

St Catherine's Roman Catholic Church was built on the western side of West Drayton Green in 1869. The original design of the church included a tower but funds did not allow this to be finished; it was finally completed in 1985.

West Drayton golf course in the early 1900s. The golf club, which was founded in 1895, had an 18-hole course on an area of 80 acres, part of which was West Drayton racecourse which flourished in the 1870s. The golf club continued until the First World War when it was forced to close.

The Garden City, *c.* 1930. This housing estate was built in the 1920s on the site of the old golf course, one road being named Fairway Avenue. The railway can be seen in the background.

The Rotary Photographic Company, *c.* 1910. The company opened in Colham Mill Road in 1900 and prospered in the early years of the century with the popularity of the picture postcard. These two publicity photographs show: (top) delivery carts, which actually belonged to the Great Western Railway but the print has been modified to show the Company's name; and (bottom) the interior of the print room.

The Closes, *c*. 1930. This path between a double row of trees formed a direct link between the churches of West Drayton and Harmondsworth and is thought to be part of a Roman trackway which ran from St Albans to Staines. The trees fell victim to Dutch Elm disease and were felled in 1975 but have since been replaced.

Station Road, early 1930s. The road from the junction of Sipson Road with Harmondsworth Road was widened at this period. The grounds of Drayton Hall (*see* p. 43) are on the left and St Martin's Vicarage is behind the trees in the centre. The vicarage has since gone but its wrought iron gates, which were fixed into the new brick wall when the road was widened, remain.

The Signal public house, Station Road, early 1930s. This was built at the turn of the century with its lower half of glazed red brick, and stood opposite the much older Six Bells. It was demolished when the road was widened in 1938.

Patrons of the Six Bells assembling for an outing, Station Road, c. 1920. The Six Bells probably dated from the seventeenth century and was demolished in the 1930s when it was replaced with the present building with the same name.

The GWR station at West Drayton, looking towards Hayes and London, 1897. The station was built in 1879 to replace the original one of 1838 which was situated about a quarter of a mile to the west. The widely spaced tracks on the right are a reminder that until 1892 they had additional rails to carry broad-gauge trains. The station remained substantially unchanged until 1983 when alterations were made; now only the buildings on the left survive largely intact.

The approach to West Drayton station, early 1900s. The horse-drawn four-wheeled cabs were the taxis of the time.

The rebuilding of the railway bridge, 6 March 1960. The steel girder bridge carrying the railway over the main road through West Drayton and Yiewsley was replaced in 1960 by the present reinforced concrete structure.

Eight members of the GWR staff at West Drayton station, *c.* 1900. Unfortunately it has not proved possible to identify any of those present.

Locomotive no. 4945 'Millington Hall' photographed on a misty morning in August 1960; it has just passed through West Drayton station and is approaching Bourne's Bridge, Hayes, heading a train of empty coaches towards London. The houses on the Bourne Avenue estate can be seen in the background. The tracks at this site are now (1996) being realigned to form Airport Junction for the projected Paddington to Heathrow Service.

YIEWSLEY

The De Burgh Arms, c. 1920. The building dates from the seventeenth century and over the years it has been much altered. However, few changes have been made since this photograph was taken.

Wooden Row, Stockley, *c*. 1935. These cottages were built for the workers in the Stockley brickfields and were situated between the canal and Stockley in the parish of Yiewsley. This settlement was called Starveall until 1912 when it was renamed because of its associations with the making of stock bricks. The cottages were removed as part of the slum clearance schemes of the 1930s.

The Forester's Arms, Stockley, 1992. The only public house in Stockley had remained substantially unchanged since it was built in the late nineteenth century. It was demolished soon after the photograph was taken. The new buildings in Stockley Park can be seen in the background.

These two photographs show the Duke of Norfolk's visit to the district to present the Viscount Bledisloe Cup. This was awarded during the Second World War to the body making the biggest contribution to the Dig for Victory campaign. In 1943 it was won by the Yiewsley and West Drayton UDC and the top photograph shows the Duke presenting the cup to Wilfred Roberts, Chairman of the Council. As part of the proceedings the Duke was presented with a bunch of onions (bottom photograph), which seems a poor exchange.

Patrons assembling outside the Red Cow, High Street, early 1920s. The Red Cow was a nineteenth-century public house which was demolished and replaced with a modern building with the same name in 1963.

The Barge School, *c.* 1935. In 1930 the Grand Union Canal Co. provided a school for the children of the canal workers on the barge *Elsdale*, anchored at Yiewsley. It was moved to Bulls Bridge, Hayes, in 1939. The top photograph shows the children boarding the barge in the morning; the bottom photograph shows the interior of the schoolroom.

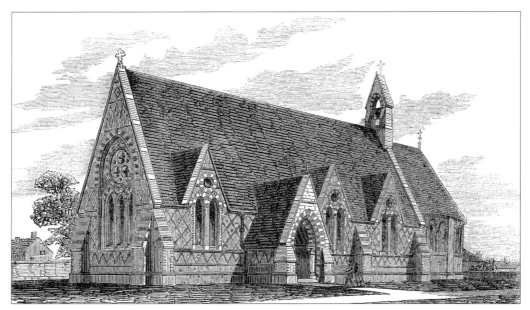

An early drawing of St Matthew's Church which was built to the design of Sir George Gilbert Scott in 1859 as a chapel within Hillingdon parish. In 1874 a separate ecclesiastical parish of Yiewsley was established and St Matthew's became the parish church. It was enlarged in 1898.

Church Rooms, Trout Road. Built in 1908 these were associated with St Matthew's Church.

Yiewsley Baptist Tabernacle, at the corner of Ernest Road (Colham Avenue) and Providence Road, was opened in 1900. It is shown here in about 1930.

Ernest Road (later Colham Avenue), *c.* 1920. The central area, planted with trees, was a branch of the canal until 1912 and was known as Otter Dock.

The Chequers, Trout Road, *c.* 1905. Built in the seventeenth or early eighteenth century, The Chequers was an established inn by 1739 and by 1822 was known as The Trout. It was very popular with anglers and some time after 1916 was renamed The Trout and Chequers. It closed in about 1950 and was later demolished.

Harman's Beer House, Horton Road, *c.* 1920. Miss Phoebe Rumble, the licensee, stands near the gate. The beer house was near the canal.

The approach to Colham Bridge, *c.* 1930. This view of the bridge shows the traffic difficulties that were caused by the steep approach and sharp bends where the High Street crosses the canal. Collins Brothers' bakery is on the right and on the left is The Anchor public house (on the other side of the canal).

The southern end of High Street, *c.* 1925. This view, looking north, shows the canal bridge and Johnson's Wax factory (Colham Wharf) in the distance. On the right are shops, which have survived, then occupied by W.H. Smiths and the pharmacy of Luty Wells. The entrance to the station approach road is on the right.

Colham Bridge, *c*. 1900. The original bridge, dating from 1794, which carried Yiewsley High Street over the canal was known as Colham Bridge. It was Bridge no. 192 of the Grand Junction Canal. The large warehouse on the left is Colham Wharf, dated 1796, and on the right is The Anchor public house. This bridge was replaced by a steel girder bridge early in the twentieth century. The bottom photograph is a view from Colham Bridge looking north along the High Street.

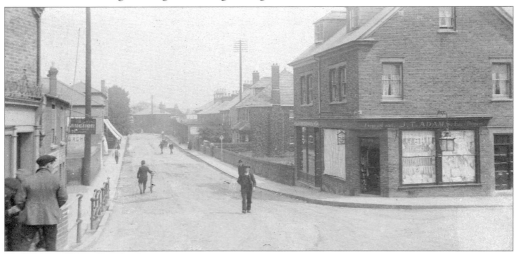

Colham Bridge, *c.* 1920. This steel girder bridge replaced the earlier brick bridge (*see* p. 63) and was itself replaced by the present reinforced concrete structure in 1939.

Aerial view of Yiewsley, looking north, 1939. This shows the reconstruction of Colham Bridge with a temporary bridge on the right.

High Street, *c.* 1900. This view, looking north, was photographed from outside what is now Woolworths. The entrance to St Matthew's Church can be seen on the left and to Fairfield Road on the right.

Evelyn's School, Apple Tree Avenue, 1937. The school opened on 11 March 1936 with accommodation for about 800 children. This photograph shows a PT class for boys, typical of the period.

A contingent of WAAFs (Women's Auxiliary Air Force) marching past Yiewsley Town Hall during a Wings for Victory Parade in 1943. During the Second World War the government launched campaigns from time to time to encourage the public to help the war effort by increasing their National Savings contributions. Wings for Victory was one such campaign which contributed to the purchase of more aircraft for the RAF.

Coronation procession, Yiewsley High Street, 1937. The procession was to celebrate the coronation of King George VI in May 1937.

Pig food collection, Castle Avenue, *c*. 1943. One of the features of life in the Second World War was the collection of kitchen waste for use as pig food; this was organized by the local authority. The food is being collected in a road-sweeper's barrow.

HARLINGTON

The Dower House, High Street, 1958. This house dates from the sixteenth century and is, apart from the church, probably the oldest building in Harlington. It is basically half-timbered with a late eighteenth-century brick front. The porch shown here was a later addition and was subsequently removed on the grounds that it was not in the correct style for the age of the building.

Aerial view of Harlington (right, centre) and Sipson (left, centre), 1949. Harmondsworth is just off the left hand side. The built-up areas of Hayes and West Drayton are beginning to encroach at the top of the photograph but the villages are, as yet, largely undisturbed by Heathrow Airport which can be seen under construction at the bottom. Agriculture is still the main industry and the land is under intensive cultivation. The patch-work pattern of the fields closely follows the pattern laid down by the Enclosure Acts of over one hundred years earlier (Harmondsworth 1819 and Harlington 1821).

(Photograph courtesy of Aerofilms)

Harlington Church. The church is by far the oldest building in Harlington. This is one of the earliest known views of the church (1794) and is interesting in that it shows the north side of the church before the north aisle was added in 1880. There is no reason to doubt the accuracy of the drawing, although the two yew trees are wildly out of proportion. Below: this 1879 painting by Josiah Parlby shows the south side of the church prior to the restoration in 1880. Before the restoration, the exterior of the church was entirely covered with plaster, except for the tower; during the restoration the plaster was removed to reveal the flint. The painting gives a more accurate impression of the two yews.

The Harlington Yew, 1810. An earlier (1770) print of the tree, on the southern side of the church, shows it to have been cut into an even more fantastic shape. A doggerel rhyme about the tree, written in 1729, gave its dimensions as over 40 ft high; it was regularly reshaped as part of the annual Whitsun village fair. The clipping ceased in 1825 and the tree was allowed to revert to its natural shape. The tree, which even in 1729 was said to be hollow, collapsed during a gale in 1959. However, the stump recovered and the tree is still growing vigorously. It is clearly several hundred years old and could well be even older than the church.

This painting by M. Dessurne shows the church and northern end of Harlington village in the early 1880s. The church is unchanged in appearance but the cedar tree behind the tower has grown somewhat in the intervening one hundred years. The thatched roof of Pear Tree Cottage on the left was later replaced with slates before the building was demolished in the 1930s. The black barn next to the house survived until 1960.

Harlington Rectory, 1969. Parts of the old Rectory on the north side of the church dated from the sixteenth century but the main part (shown here) was an attractive Victorian building. The Rectory was demolished in 1970 and most of the trees cut down to make way for a housing estate which spoilt the previously attractive setting of the ancient parish church.

Dawley House, *c*. 1700. The Domesday Survey (1086) mentions the existence of two manors within the parish: Harlington (Herdintone) itself and Dawley (Dallega). For much of their history the two manors were in common ownership with the lord of both manors choosing to live in Dawley House. By 1600 Dawley as a separate hamlet had virtually ceased to exist as a result of the acquisition of land around the manor house. In 1607 the manors of Harlington and Dawley were acquired by Sir John Bennet and the manors remained with the family until they were sold by Charles Bennet jnr in 1724. This engraving shows the manor house, and the large park that had been created around it, when it was occupied by Charles Bennet snr (1674–1722), Lord Ossulstone (later the Earl of Tankerville). In his diary, Samuel Pepys mentions that he passed 'my Lord Arlington's House that he was born in a towne called Harlington'. Henry Bennet (1618–85), later Lord (H)Arlington, was the uncle of Charles Bennet snr but, although he did indeed at one time live at Dawley House, he was not born there.

Dawley House in the early 1930s. The old Dawley House (*see* p. 74) was pulled down and the new one, which had been started by Charles Bennet, Earl of Tankerville, was sold in 1724 to Henry St John, Viscount Bolingbroke, for whom it was remodelled by James Gibbs. Most of this house was demolished in the late eighteenth century but the building shown here, which had been the dairy, survived and inherited the name Dawley House. With the rest of the Dawley estate it was acquired by the De Salis family who sold it to the Gramophone Company Ltd (EMI) in 1929. It was pulled down by the company in the early 1950s.

Dawley Manor Farm, photographed from 'The Moats' recreation ground, 1961. This sixteenth-century building was one of the oldest and most attractive of the farmhouses that stood in the village High Street. It survived for only 18 months after this photograph was taken and was the only building in Harlington to be destroyed by the construction of the M4 motorway.

Construction of the M4 motorway through Harlington began in late 1962. Typically, no consideration whatever was given to any adverse environmental effects that this would cause, and the cheapest solution was chosen throughout the length of its construction. In Harlington this meant the closure of the old High Street and the construction of a diversion to cross the M4 by means of a bridge. These two 1963 photographs show the dreadful effect of this decision. The top photograph shows the construction of the embankment to take the realigned High Street over the motorway. The bottom photograph shows Bedwell Gardens, which had been a quiet cul-de-sac, but became a main road with traffic passing at bedroom-window height. For very little extra cost the motorway could have been built in a cutting with all roads crossing it at ground level.

Jessop's Pond, High Street, early 1900s. This photograph was taken from outside Dawley Manor Farm looking north. The trees on the right, to the north of the pond, occupy the site of what is now the fire station. The pond formed part of Frog's Ditch which runs through 'The Moats' on the opposite side of the road. It was filled in in the 1930s following an accident in which a motor-cyclist was drowned. In the early nineteenth century Dawley Manor Farm was occupied by Joseph Jessop, hence the name.

Harlington Cricket Club, c. 1914. The man standing on the extreme left is Robert Newman, who was President of the club from 1898 until his death in 1925. His son Robert and his brother Charles are on the left in the back row; none of the others has been identified. At the time, the club played on land belonging to R. Newman, between Dawley Manor Farm and Church Farm. In the early 1900s the most notable member of the club was J.W. (Jack) Hearne who later played for Middlesex and England.

The unveiling of the War Memorial, 1921. Seventy-five men from Harlington were killed in the First World War. A memorial tablet was placed on the wall inside the church in 1920 and the memorial cross in the churchyard was unveiled on 18 August 1921. An additional 44 names were added to the memorial after the Second World War, and another one after the Korean War in 1953. This photograph, taken from the bedroom window of Church Farm, shows the cross being unveiled by the Chaplain General, Bishop Taylor Smith. The other clergyman is Herbert Wilson, Rector from 1905 to 1929.

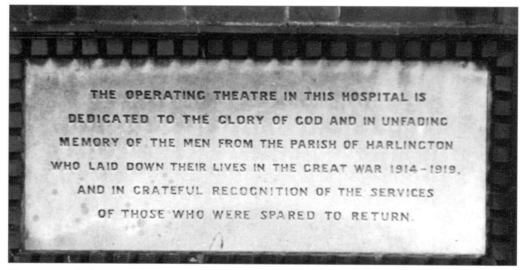

War memorial plaque in the Cottage Hospital, Sipson Lane. In addition to the war memorial in the churchyard, an operating theatre, paid for by public subscription in 'unfading' memory of the war dead, was built as an extension to the Cottage Hospital. Memories soon fade, however, and the Cottage Hospital, together with the operating theatre, has been sold to an Asian religious group and the plaque is now completely hidden behind shrubs. (*See* p. 87)

Church Farm, 1958. As its name suggests, this farmhouse stood immediately opposite the church. It was a T-shaped, timber-framed house with a brick front which had been added in the eighteenth century. After it became unoccupied it was vandalized; as a result it became unsafe and had to be pulled down in 1969.

Alf Connell, greengrocer, with his delivery cart outside Church Villa, High Street, c. 1920. Church Villa was the house behind the railings and at this time it housed a private school run by Miss Stone. It stood on the south side of Lansdowne House and was demolished in the 1930s. Alf Connell had a shop in Chapel Row, next to the old Baptist Church (see p. 88).

Cherry Lane, early 1900s. The fragment of Cherry Lane which remains at the Harlington end was renamed St Paul's Close when the lane was cut in two by the construction of the M4 motorway in 1963. The photograph shows Dave Philp of Veysey's Farm (*see* below) in his milk float, accompanied by Master W. Warner, just outside the Rectory gate. The trees were cut down and replaced by some barrack-like houses in the early 1970s.

Veysey's Farm, High Street, 1970. This early nineteenth-century farmhouse was, presumably, named after its original owner but nothing is known about him. At the turn of the century it was occupied by David Philp, who described himself as a 'cow-keeper'. It remained as a farm until it became Crouch's woodyard and, it must be admitted, something of an eyesore. It was demolished in 1972 to make way for the houses in Bletchmore Close.

Bletchmore, High Street, 1970. Bletchmore was one of the many large houses belonging to local farmers which once lined the High Street; only Lansdowne House now remains. Bletchmore was one of the last to be built, by a member of the Philp family in whose possession it remained until its demolition in 1972. The site of the house and its large garden is now occupied by the houses in Bletchmore Close.

Vine House and Philp's baker's shop, High Street, early 1900s. At this time Vine House was the home of William Philp of W. & S. Philp, who were local farmers. They also ran the baker's shop adjoining the house, which had been in the family since at least 1851. Pear Tree Cottage (*see* p. 73) is on the extreme right.

Strawberry pickers, *c.* 1906. A wide range of tree- and soft fruits was grown in the locality. The top photograph shows a party of women from Shropshire setting off from Heyward's Farm (*see* p. 92) to pick strawberries from a field in Sipson Lane. Fruit picking is a seasonal activity and the female labour force came annually from Shropshire for the strawberry picking season. Most of these women, known locally as 'Shroppies', were pit girls from the Dawley (now Telford) area of Shropshire who regarded their visits to the fruit gardens of West Middlesex as a summer holiday with pay. The bottom photograph shows a group of strawberry pickers at the farm of W. & S. Philp. Most of these are probably local women, although they are much better dressed than was usually the case. The woman on the left of the front row is Sarah Anne Lee, but the others have not been identified.

Lansdowne Cottages, Brickfields Lane, 1968. These cottages were built in 1878 on the south side of the road. They were demolished soon after the photograph was taken and replaced by council housing. They were owned by Robert Newman of Lansdowne House, which explains the origin of their name.

Eastfield Cottages, Brickfields Lane, 1968. This pair of cottages stood alone at the far end of Brickfields Lane, and originally must have been the only houses in the lane. They derived their name from one of the pre-Enclosure (1821) open fields of the parish. The similarly named Westfield Cottages in Sipson Lane still remain.

The White Hart, 1916. Since this photograph was taken two extensions have been added to the north side of the building. The original wing is still easily identifiable and dates from 1810, although there was a pub with the same name on the site before this. The licensee from 1914 to 1928 was William Dolan and his daughter Eileen is at the upstair window. The car is a model T Ford chassis with a special body for carrying extra passengers.

Children at the National School, c. 1920. Harlington and Cranford National School was opened in 1848 by the church authorities of the two parishes. In 1883 a separate school was opened for the children of Cranford, so most of the children in the photograph would have come from Harlington but none has been identified.

The National School, High Street, 1958. The school stood in the High Street next to the site now used by the Harlington Locomotive Society. It was closed in July 1939 and the children transferred to the newly opened William Byrd school on the Bath Road. The school building was then used for industrial purposes until it was demolished in 1962.

William Byrd School, Bath Road, 1939. As a result of the rapid growth in the population of the district in the 1930s, Middlesex County Council built a new school which they named after William Byrd, the Elizabethan composer who lived in Harlington between 1577 and 1593. The school opened in 1939 and closed in 1974 when the children were transferred to the new school of the same name in Victoria Lane. (Photograph courtesy of *Uxbridge Gazette* series of newspapers)

The Forge, High Street, *c.* 1905. Most villages at this time had a forge but Harlington had two. This one was on the west side of the High Street between the Red Lion and the White Hart. By the early 1960s it had ceased to be a forge and the buildings were demolished in the 1980s.

The centre of the village, the Red Lion crossroads, where High Street, Sipson Lane and Cranford Lane met, photographed in 1958. The large white house, known as Gothic House, had been converted from what had previously been a group of cottages. It was demolished in the early 1960s and the site is now occupied by Gothic Court.

Cottage Hospital, Sipson Lane, early 1900s. The Harlington, Harmondsworth and Cranford Cottage Hospital was opened in 1884 as a joint venture by the three parish councils. This is the back of the building before the extensions which were added in the 1920s. The hospital was closed in 1974 and the building sold by the Hillingdon Health Authority. It is now owned by the 'Sant Nirankari Mandal Universal Brotherhood'.

Poplar House, High Street, 1961. This attractive, early nineteenth-century house was demolished in the early 1970s and replaced by an ugly block of flats known as Felbridge Court. The single-storey building attached to the house was a later addition and served as a grocer's shop until it was demolished.

Old Baptist Church, *c. 1880*. Originally built in 1770, this building has been added to at various dates and the dissenting group which met there became Baptists in 1798. Once described as 'the ugliest building in the village' it has since had to relinquish the title in the face of strong competition from more recent developments. In 1879 the new Baptist Church was built immediately opposite and the old building was used for meetings and lectures. In 1975 the side extensions were removed and after renovation it was renamed 'The Frank Peace Hall' in memory of a former Baptist Minister.

The new Baptist Church, *c. 1935*. After adding several extensions to their old church, the Baptists ran out of space and in 1879 opened a new church just across the road. The village pond is in the foreground.

Manor Farm and Chapel Row (left), *c.* 1920. Manor Farm was demolished in the 1930s and replaced with the shops in Manor Parade. Chapel Row was demolished in the 1950s and replaced with a row of houses at the same angle to the High Street. Snow clearing is in progress, with the snow being deposited in the pond just out of picture to the left. The circular area in the middle of the picture was originally the village animal pound.

The Lilacs, High Street, 1961. This house stood beside the village pond and was reputedly the home of William Byrd when he lived in Harlington (1577–93). The house was old enough for this to be true but there is no evidence of Byrd's occupancy. In the mid-nineteenth century it had been a private school for boys, called Overburg House. It was demolished in 1968. The name Turpins on the plate in the foreground refers to the adjoining eighteenth-century house which still remains.

The Original Wheatsheaf and Wheatsheaf Cottages, High Street. In the top photograph, taken in about 1910, Ferris's butcher's shop partially obscures the public house known as the Original Wheatsheaf, so named to distinguish it from the (new) Wheatsheaf almost immediately opposite. The buildings to the left of the photograph still stand. The two public houses continued to trade in competition with each other for some considerable time before the older building was converted into the cottages shown here in about 1930. The signboard of the original public house has been removed but the support for it left in place. The site is now occupied by Stor-a-Cars and part of the walls of the old building are still standing.

Sunnyside Cottages, High Street, *c.* 1910. This row of nine cottages was known locally as the Nine Houses, but an earlier name was Sapperton Row. Beyond the cottages, which were demolished in 1958, is one of the barns of Heyward's Farm. The large building, extreme right, still remains.

The southern end of High Street, taken from the junction of West End Lane with the High Street, looking north, *c.* 1904. On the right is the barn of Heyward's Farm; Sunnyside Cottages (seen in the previous picture) are in the middle distance with the Baptist Church and The Manse in the far distance.

The Elms and Heyward's Farm, High Street, *c.* 1916. The house was at the time the home of Ebenezer Heyward, owner of one of the largest farms in the area. The farmyard (below) stood on the northern side of the house. The man on the right is Ebenezer Heyward himself, with his three elder daughters Jessie, Poppy and Doris.

Shooting party, 1906. These desperate-looking characters are not a local vigilante group, but are enjoying the annual shooting event that took place on Boxing Day. Most of the group were local farmers. Boys (left to right): Stanley Heyward, Jack Heyward, Sidney Heyward, -?-. Second row: Ebenezer Heyward, William Philp, Robert Newman, Richard Heyward, John Heyward, Sam Philp. Back row: -?-, Herbert Tyler, Fred Philp, Art Philp, -?-, -?-, Bert Philp, R.P.Newman, ? Curtis, -?-, -?-, -?-.

Elder Farm, West End Lane, 1958. The only possible contender for the title of the oldest domestic building in Harlington dates, as does the Dower House, from the sixteenth century. In the 1930s it was known as Garner's Cottages and was divided into tenements. The original timber-framed part of the building (at right angles to the road) is now rendered and pebble-dashed but nevertheless still shows some traces of its former construction.

The Coach and Horses, and Ariel Hotel, 1961. The Coach and Horses at Harlington Corner was an eighteenth-century coaching inn and well known landmark but this did not save it from destruction when the Ariel Hotel was built behind it in 1961. This photograph was taken just before the old inn was demolished, and shows that there was no real need for its destruction. Confusingly, the hotel has since been renamed The Post House, whilst the hotel formerly of that name is now The Forte Crest.

Harlington Hall, shortly before demolition, 1955. This mid-Victorian house stood on the north side of the Bath Road at Harlington Corner, opposite the Coach and Horses. After its demolition the site remained vacant for many years but is now occupied by an office block known as Capital Place.

The Cedars and Hatton Gore, Hatton Road. Prior to the Enclosure in 1821, the segment of Harlington parish that lay south of the Bath Road formed part of Harlington Common, and hence none of the buildings in this part of Harlington could have pre-dated 1821 but a number of fairly large houses appeared soon after, two of which are shown here. The Cedars (above) was at one time the home of Mary Ann Cooper (née Mitton), who was the inspiration of Charles Dickens' character 'Little Dorrit'. As a friend of the family Charles Dickens was a regular visitor. The drawing of Hatton Gore (below) is from a sales leaflet of 1838. The middle part of the house remained basically unaltered until it was demolished in 1945. In the 1930s the house was the home of Frank Kingdon Ward (1885–1958), a famous plant collector. He constructed a rock garden, designing it to look like a bend in a river ravine in the Himalayas. It was built from York stone acquired from the demolition of the old Bank of England building. During the war the house was occupied by the Welsh Guards and briefly, before it was demolished, by the Home Guard.

Police station, Bath Road, 1946. The police station stood on the south side of the Bath Road, opposite to the junction with New Road. It opened in 1890 and closed in 1965 when the constabulary transferred to West Drayton. The building was sold to BAA in 1967 and was demolished soon after. The air-raid siren on the roof was installed in 1938.

The Pheasant, West End Lane, 1969. This building dates from the mid-eighteenth century and is now the oldest public house in Harlington. Since the photograph was taken the exterior, although basically unchanged, has been tarted up with consequent damage to its appearance.

HARMONDSWORTH – WITH HEATHROW, LONGFORD & SIPSON

Harmondsworth Church, 1792. The exterior of the church has changed little in the intervening years but, apart from the tower, little can now be seen from the road because of the trees that have grown in the intervening years. This print therefore gives a much better impression of the church than can be gained from any modern photograph.

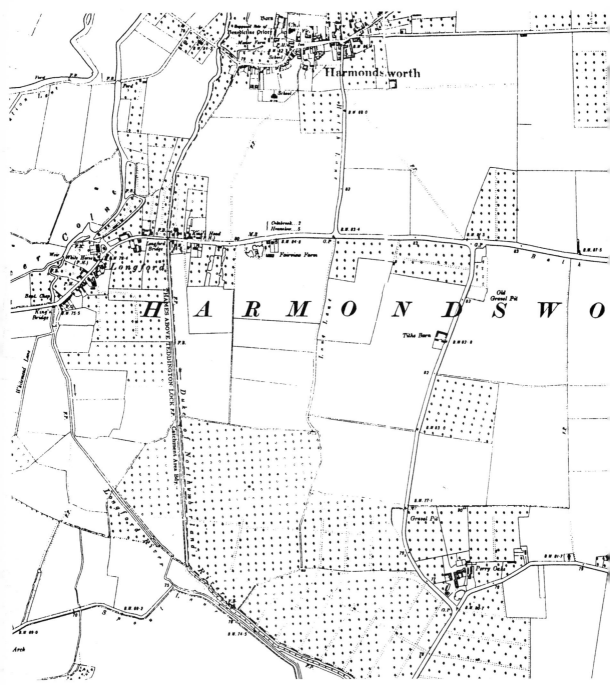

Harlington–Harmondsworth area, c. 1912. At this time all the land between the still small villages of Harlington, Sipson, Harmondsworth, Longford and Heathrow was given over to market gardening and fruit growing. Between the wars Harlington, Sipson and Harmondsworth grew in size but still retained their village characters, while Longford and Heathrow hardly changed. Agriculture remained the

predominant activity but was delivered a mortal blow when all the area to the south of the Bath Road was requisitioned in 1944 for the development of Heathrow Airport, under the pretext that it was needed as an RAF base.

Harmondsworth Manor House, 1794. The original sixteenth-century Manor House is said to have been pulled down in 1774 and the name transferred to this half-timbered building. The present Manor Farm House, probably on the same site near the barn, dates from the early nineteenth century.

The west side of the Great Barn *c*. 1920. 'The finest medieval barn in the country', according to Sir John Betjeman, is also one of the largest, measuring 191 ft in length, 28 ft in width and 39 ft in height. Impressive, by virtue of its size, from the outside, the interior is magnificent and has been likened to a 'cathedral in wood'. It dates from the early fifteenth century and was built at a time when the manor of Harmondsworth was owned by Winchester College.

The firemen and fire engine of Harmondsworth fire brigade, in front of the Gable Stores, *c.* 1880. The driver of the engine is William Hissey. Seated (left to right): Isaac Blondell (also sexton and gravedigger), W. Belch, D. Nicholls. Standing: H.C. Belch (chief and father of W. Belch), Tom Truss (also village blacksmith), Samuel Bateman (later to become chief). At the window is Mrs Sophia Ashby. The fire engine, which still exists, was renovated in 1905 and bears the inscription 'Harmondsworth 1905'.

'The Sun, Cork Club, 1913' is the caption on the photograph but it is not clear what the Cork Club was nor what it did. The Sun Inn dates from the sixteenth century; at the time of the photograph only half was used as a pub, the other half being a butcher's shop. The whole building was later converted into a house (Sun House) but the hooks used by the butcher are still in position.

Two views of the centre of Harmondsworth. In the top photograph, looking east in about 1910, are the Elizabethan cottages (extreme right) which were demolished in 1937, and to their left is The Crown. Opposite is the Vicarage Hall and beyond Blacksmith's Row; The Lodge can be seen in the far distance. In the bottom photograph, looking west in about 1920, is the Gable Stores and the half-timbered cottages on the left. Between them and the Five Bells, on the extreme right, is the entrance to Moor Lane. Standing on the village green to the right of the children is a captured German cannon. This cannon was placed in position soon after the end of the First World War, but it was soon relocated to Harmondsworth recreation ground; it remained there until the Second World War when it was removed, as were the iron railings around the church, during the campaign to salvage scrap metal.

The Five Bells and Sun House, *c.* 1920. The seventeenth-century Five Bells stands opposite the church and, at the time that the house was given its name, the church did indeed have five bells, although a sixth bell has since been added. Except for the fact that the village centre now has severe parking problem this scene has remained largely unchanged in the last 70 years.

Village centre, *c.* 1965. Most of the buildings seen in the earlier photographs remain, with the sad exception of the half-timbered cottages. Thirty years on the view is still much the same but is now completely ruined by indiscriminate parking.

Blacksmith's Row, 1935. This group of terraced cottages was named from the forge which adjoined them. They were demolished in 1937 as part of the slum clearance scheme. The decorations are to celebrate the Silver Jubilee of King George V.

Junction of Holloway Lane and Harmondsworth Lane at the eastern end of the village, 1936. These two roads lead to West Drayton and Sipson respectively. At the junction stood the early seventeenth-century Centre House, which was demolished in the early 1960s.

Moor Lane, looking west, 1935. This photograph was taken just before most of the houses in the lane were demolished as part of the slum clearance programme. The houses which replaced them were built immediately to the rear. A house very similar to the gabled house in the foreground still remains at the village end of the lane

Duke's Bridge, *c*. 1910. Moor Lane continues in a westerly direction to cross three rivers. The first of these is Northumberland's River, hence the name of the bridge. This bridge, which still stands, was the only proper bridge in Moor Lane at the time. The house in the background has long since disappeared; the caption on the photograph describes it as 'Dick Turpin's Cottage'. Despite popular legend, there is no evidence that Dick Turpin ever visited the district.

Thomas Wild jnr of Sipson posing on the footbridge over the River Colne, Harmondsworth Moor, *c.* 1910. From the Duke's Bridge, Moor Lane continued over the River Colne and the Wraysbury River, both of which were crossed by wooden footbridges of the type shown here. The bridges were only three planks in width, with gaps between the planks which made cycling across them a foolhardy venture.

Stones from Waterloo Bridge, Harmondsworth Moor, 1936. The decision to demolish the old Waterloo Bridge, which had been designed by John Rennie snr and built between 1811 and 1817, rather than to attempt its restoration, was highly controversial. To placate the critics, each stone was numbered and the stones were transported by road to a site on Harmondsworth Moor for 'temporary' storage. It was claimed that this would allow the eventual re-erection of the bridge on another site. Of course this never happened; some of the stones were used by an enterprising company set up nearby to make stone fireplaces, but most of those that remained were crushed to provide aggregate for use as roadbase for the M25 motorway in the mid-1980s.

Road Research Laboratory, Colnbrook by-pass, 1940s. The laboratory started life in 1930 as the Ministry of Transport Experimental Station. Three years later it become the Road Research Laboratory, as a separate station of the Department of Scientific and Industrial Research. The Harmondsworth Laboratory, which was concerned with the design and construction of roads, opened a Road Safety Division at Langley in 1945. As the work expanded, both sites became too small and in 1966 all the activities were transferred to a new laboratory at Crowthorne in Berkshire. The old buildings are now known as 'Government Offices, Harmondsworth' and among other things houses an immigration detention centre.

Colnbrook by-pass, 1951. The absence of traffic meant that the photographer could stand in the middle of the road in complete safety. By 1965 the traffic had increased to 28,500 vehicles a day, a number that fell by two-thirds when the M4 was opened. The patchwork pattern on the road is caused by experimental surfacing laid by the Road Research Laboratory.

The new Peggy Bedford and Colnbrook by-pass, *c*. 1929. This aerial view shows the recently constructed Peggy Bedford and the eastern end of the by-pass still under construction.

The junction of Bath Road and Colnbrook by-pass after completion. The new Peggy Bedford, at the junction of the old Bath Road and the new by-pass, became a well known local landmark but was demolished in 1995 to make way for a drive-in restaurant and petrol service station.

The old Peggy Bedford, Longford, early 1930s. This public house, formerly the King's Head, derived its name from the lady who was the licensee for more than fifty years before her death in 1859. It closed when the new inn of the same name opened in 1930 and soon afterwards the front of the old inn was destroyed by fire. The back part survived and with a new front added has become a private house known as The Stables.

Rear view of the old Peggy Bedford, Longford, 1921. The old Peggy Bedford was a T-shaped building, with the top of the T fronting the old Bath Road. When the top of the T was destroyed this part was largely undamaged and comparison of this photograph with the present building shows that it still survives, the main differences being that the half-timbering has been exposed and additional windows added. One of the bricks in the wall on the other side of the rear of what is now The Stables, bears the inscription 'TMA 1691'.

Hunt's Cottage, Longford, 1935. This is the caption on the photograph, although the house is better known as the Quaker Meeting House. It stands on the south side of the Bath Road, almost opposite the old Peggy Bedford, and was used by the Quakers from 1676 until it was sold by them in 1875. It has remained since then as a private house.

The Square, Longford, early 1900s. The part of the village around the White Horse was known as The Square. Most of the buildings shown here remain: just behind the public house is White's Farm, which now (1996) has a thatched roof. The bricked-up windows of the White Horse recall the window tax which was introduced in 1696 and not repealed until 1851.

The Farm, Longford, *c.* 1907. The house dated from about 1830 and was the home of H.J. Wild of H.J. Wild & Sons. He came to Longford in the 1860s to help his uncle Richard Weekly, who had been incapacitated after being struck by lightning whilst sitting by the fireplace in Weekly House. The two little girls – Peggy and Betty – are the daughters of his eldest son William, who lived in Weekly House, just out of view to the right. The farmhouse has been demolished and replaced, and together with the converted Weekly House now forms a small office complex.

Longford Baptist Chapel, *c.* 1950. In 1859 Richard Weekly built the Zoar Baptist Chapel on the side of one of his cottages, chiefly for the benefit of the elderly and infirm. The name of the chapel was later changed from Zoar to Zion. By the time this photograph was taken no changes in its appearance had occurred but it was no longer in use as a chapel. The building has since been modified and incorporated into the adjoining house.

King's Bridge, Longford, *c.* 1910. This bridge is so-called because the Crown is responsible for its upkeep; the river which it bridges is an artificial channel which was cut in the reign of Charles I to improve the water supply to Hampton Court. The bridge has the monogram 'W.IV.R 1834' on its parapet. To the left are Florence Villas and in the distance The King's Arms.

Mad Bridge, Longford, 1970. This scene had barely changed for seventy years, but the construction of the M25 motorway has changed it beyond recognition. Mad Bridge crosses the Wraysbury River, which at this point forms the western boundary of Harmondsworth parish. The origin of the name of the bridge is not known; it may be a corruption of 'Mead' Bridge but in view of what has happened in its vicinity, 'Mad' is very apt.

Vinery Cottages, Sipson Road, at the north end of Sipson village, *c.* 1910. These cottages were built by Thomas Wild for his farm workers in 1888 and derived their name from the Vineries (*see* p. 115), where he lived. Because there were nine pairs of cottages they were known locally as the Eighteen Row. The two pairs of cottages nearest the camera were badly damaged by a bomb in late 1940 and had to be demolished – the only significant bomb damage suffered by Sipson. The remainder were demolished in the early 1960s and nos 241–265 Sipson Road erected on the site.

Sipson Baptist Church, *c.* 1900. This began life in 1891 as a Salvation Army Hall; in 1897 it became a Gospel Mission Hall and in 1901 it was enlarged to its present size. It became a Baptist Church on 19 September 1905. The building was converted into residential accommodation in the mid-1980s but the external appearance was largely maintained. Church services are now held in what was formerly the Sunday School rooms.

Sipson Farm, 1969. At the turn of the century various branches of the Wild family were farming in the area, the most successful business being that of Thomas Wild and Son of Sipson Farm. In 1898 Thomas Wild took a junior partner, Rowland Robbins, to form the firm of Wild and Robbins which became the best known farming enterprise in the district. It was based at Sipson Farm and the large farm buildings shown here give an indication of its prosperity. The farm survived until the early 1970s and the farm buildings were pulled down to make way for housing about ten years later.

Female farm workers, Sipson Farm, early 1900s. Much of the work in the fields was carried out by a female labour-force, referred to as field women. They used sacks as aprons and to cover their heads. Those seen here are working in the fields between Sipson Road and Holloway Lane.

The Vineries, *c.* 1905. The large house on the left was built in about 1880 for Thomas Wild, who had previously lived in the old Sipson Farmhouse, a seventeenth-century building which stood between The Vineries and Sipson Farm. On coming to Sipson R.R. Robbins lived in the old farmhouse which was demolished when he moved to Hollycroft in the early 1900s. The Vineries was demolished in 1970 and the site is now occupied by the houses in Vineries Close. The roof of the Baptist Church (*see* p. 113) can be seen to the right of the house. Across the road are some old cottages which were demolished in 1935.

The Welcome coffee tavern, Sipson, early 1900s. The members of the Wild and Robbins families were staunch non-conformists and to discourage their workmen from drinking, The Welcome coffee tavern was opened in 1897 as a counter-attraction to public houses. Non-alcoholic drinks could be obtained in the coffee room on the left while the reading room on the right was available as a recreational room to read, play games and pass the time of day. The building was converted into two semi-detached houses in the 1930s; these were demolished in 1989.

The Homestead, *c.* 1905. This attractive seventeenth-century house stood on the north side of 'The Crown' on the site now occupied by 379–391 Sipson Road. At the time this photograph was taken it was occupied by Thomas Hood, his wife and four daughters, none of whom married. On the death of Helen Hood in 1941 ownership of the house passed to R.R. Robbins, who lived in 'Hollycroft' on the opposite side of the road. Because he considered that the house spoilt his view, he had it demolished!

Sipson post office and village store, *c.* 1935. The front part of the post office is a Victorian addition to a much older building. The rear is half-timbered and, with the possible exception of the King William public house, is the oldest building in Sipson by a considerable margin.

The van works of Wild and Robbins, Sipson, *c.* 1910. Messrs Wild and Robbins of Sipson Farm were virtually self-sufficient. They generated their own electricity, had their own water supply and their own forge, where all their horses and those of other farms were shod. They also had their own van works, where horse-drawn vehicles were made for their own use and for sale. This photograph shows their team of workmen standing outside the works with a waggon made for Smith's jam factory, which was little more than 100 yds away. Standing (left to right): F.M. Holman (foreman), 'Dibdab' Dopson, J.E. Josey, Mickey Druce, -?-, -?-, 'Joko' Dopson, Ike Littleford.

Sipson Lane, photographed from outside the Baptist Church, *c.* 1910. On the right are Appleton's Cottages which were demolished in the late 1960s, and on the left is Inglenook, then the home of Thomas Wild jnr and now a children's nursery. The trees in the distance are in the grounds of Wall Gardens Farm (*see* p. 118).

Wall Gardens Farm, Sipson Lane 1970. This farm was originally the most elaborate of the many orchards belonging to the Smith family, who owned the jam factory in Sipson. The orchard, 16 acres in extent, was surrounded by a high wall. Within this area the orchard was divided into rectangles, each of which was also surrounded by a high wall. The walls helped to protect the trees from cold winds and frost in the spring. By 1970 most of the trees had been removed. The farmhouse, barns and most of the walls still remain but the whole site is now used as a gigantic car park in flagrant disregard of planning regulations.

Sipson Way, 1935. The larger houses at the end of Sipson Way were built by Staines RDC in 1923 as part of a Government-sponsored scheme to make houses available for sale at a reasonable price. The scheme was a failure and all but two had to be offered for rent as council houses. The houses in the foreground were built later, when the opportunity was taken to link Sipson Way with the Bath Road. Before this time, Sipson Road was the only link between Sipson village and the Bath Road.

Sipson and Heathrow School, Bath Road, 1945. This school, on the north side of the Bath Road, opened as Heathrow Elementary School in 1877. By 1915 the school had changed its name to reflect the fact that it was much nearer to Sipson, where the majority of the pupils lived. The school closed in 1966 and the building was demolished soon after. Illogically its replacement, in Harmondsworth Lane, Sipson, retained the original name. The house on the right was occupied by the headmaster, Mr W.C. Knapp, but after his retirement it became the caretaker's house. (Photograph courtesy of *Uxbridge Gazette* series of newspapers)

St Saviour's Mission Hall, Bath Road, *c*. 1910. This view was taken from the junction of Sipson Road and the Bath Road, looking west. The Mission Church was a corrugated iron structure, known as the Tin Church, built to serve this part of Harmondsworth parish in 1880. It was demolished in 1934 and replaced with a brick church hall which stood further back from the road. This in turn was demolished to make way for the Excelsior Hotel in the early 1960s. To the right of the large tree can be seen the roof of Sipson and Heathrow School and opposite the tree is the Old Magpies.

Sipson House, 1969. In 1969 this fine Georgian house was still in good condition but soon after it became vacant and was purchased by BAA which allowed it to become derelict. Permission to restore it and convert it into offices was given in 1979 but the restoration involved total demolition except for the front façade. In the mid-nineteenth century the house was occupied by the Cooper family, one member of which, John Cartwright Cooper, married Mary Ann Mitton (see p. 95). The field name to the west of the house was Scroogeall which perhaps provided the inspiration for the name of the main character in *A Christmas Carol*.

Servants at Doghurst, *c.* 1900. Doghurst stood just to the east of Sipson House and gave its name to both Doghurst Drive and Doghurst Avenue. While the Coopers were living in Sipson House, Doghurst was occupied by the Mitton family, but at the time of the photograph the house was owned by Henry Harrison. Minnie Hancock is on the right in the back row, and to her right is Walter Prince whom she later married. At this time one-third of the female population was in domestic service and even comparatively modest houses such as Doghurst could employ as many as the eleven shown here.

The Old Magpies, Bath Road, 1950. The Old Magpies Inn stood on the south side of the Bath Road about 100 yds to the west of the Three Magpies. It dated from the sixteenth century and was needlessly demolished in 1951; its site was then used as a car park until 1963 when the airport spur road was built through the area. The presence of two public houses with similar names meant that this part of the parish was referred to as the Magpies. Officially it was Sipson Green but the War Memorial in Harmondsworth Church refers to it as St Saviour's, Bath Road – a name not used before or since.

The Three Magpies, Bath Road, 1921. This public house, which dates from the eighteenth century, has since been over-extensively restored and has lost its outbuildings. However, it is a unique survivor of the old coaching inns on the Bath Road near Heathrow. In 1765 it was known as the Three Pigeons and later as The Magpies and Pigeon. Standing outside is the landlord Mr Rawlings with his wife and two children, Fred and Doris.

The Air Hostess (formerly the Bricklayer's Arms), Bath Road, in 1985, shortly before demolition. The original inn on the site was the Bricklayer's Arms, which was demolished in 1928 to allow for the widening of the Bath Road. It was replaced by the building shown here which was renamed in May 1954. For some years the licence was held by J.W. (Jack) Hearne, the well known Middlesex and England cricketer. The site is now occupied by a drive-in McDonalds.

The western end of General Roy's baseline, Heathrow, 1944. The cannon was placed in position to mark the end of the baseline that had been measured across Hounslow Heath in 1784 as part of a trigonometric survey. The man in charge of these measurements was Major-General William Roy, the 'father of the Ordnance Survey'. To commemorate the 200th anniversary of his birth, a plaque was placed on top of the cannon in 1926. The cannon was removed in 1944 but later returned to its rightful place; the plaque has now been re-set in a concrete plinth at the base.

Flying at Heathrow, Cain's Lane, *c.* 1905. This is probably the earliest recorded example of any flying activity at Heathrow; it shows a lighter-than-air balloon which had made a forced landing at Cain's Farm. It clearly created much excitement and a large crowd, many with bicycles, gathered. Twenty-five years later the Fairey Aviation Company opened its airfield in Cain's Lane close to where the balloon had crash landed.

Heathrow Farm, 1936. Heathrow Road, which led from the Bath Road at the Three Magpies, was lined with old farmhouses such as this. Dating from the sixteenth century, this farmhouse was situated on the north side of Heathrow Road just beyond the junction with Cain's Lane. It was a timber-framed building, which had been refaced with brick in the eighteenth century. It was demolished in 1944.

David and John Wild with their employees (mostly land-girls), photographed just before eviction from Wild's Farm, Cains Lane, Heathrow, 1944. Left to right: Pearl Clark, Maisie Aldridge, Joanna Wilkinson, Pamela Hart, Bunny Shaw, Frank Hillier, Eric Lipscombe, Helen Hayes, Winnie Baker, Nita Walden, Elizabeth Wild (aged 5), David Wild, James Wild (aged 2½). In the cart is John Wild. The horse was called Captain.

Rear view of Perry Oaks Farm, 1936. Perry Oaks is now a well known sludge works, and is the possible site of a fifth terminal for Heathrow. Long before the date of this photograph the fine old Elizabethan red-brick Perry Oaks Farm had been almost the only building in the Perry Oaks area of Heathrow. It was demolished in 1949 in the second phase of the development of the airport.

Milk float at Cain's Farm, Heathrow, early 1900s. At this time Cain's Farm in Cain's Lane was occupied by Charles Glenie who also owned a shop – Cain's Farm Dairy – in Feltham. Milk floats such as this were the main means of delivering milk as bottled milk was still almost unknown. The milk was transported in churns, two of which can be seen on the float, from which the milkman measured out the milk into each householder's jugs, from pint and quart measures.

Ploughing match, Tithe Barn Lane, 1937. The Middlesex Agricultural and Growers Association held its annual ploughing match in the Heathrow area on 28 September 1937; it was the 99th and last to be held. The 100th match, scheduled for 1938, was postponed because of a prolonged drought, and the outbreak of war one year later meant that it had to be postponed again and the matches were never resumed. (Photograph courtesy of *Uxbridge Gazette* series of newspapers)

Ford in High Tree Lane, Heathrow, *c.* 1932. According to the map this was Goat House Tree Ford which crossed the Duke of Northumberland's River. However, it was known locally as High Tree Ford across High Tree River, and was a much-loved beauty spot for picnics and where children could paddle in the river and fish for tiddlers. The river was too deep for motorized traffic – the motorist seen here is taking the opportunity to wash his car in the river.

Fairey Aviation Airfield, early 1930s. The Great West Aerodrome of the Fairey Aviation Co. Ltd was acquired by the company in 1929. The large hangar with attached offices was the only building on the airfield, which was little more than a large grass field. The aeroplane is a de Havilland Puss Moth. At the time of its compulsory acquisition from the Company, the airfield occupied 200 acres and was bounded by Cain's Lane, Heathrow Road, High Tree Lane and the Duke of Northumberland's River.

BRITAIN IN OLD PHOTOGRAPHS

To order any of these titles please telephone our distributor, Littlehampton Book Services on 01903 721596
For a catalogue of these and our other titles please ring Regina Schinner on 01453 731114